PROCRASTINATION HABIT HACKS

Actionable Steps You Can Take to Hack Your Procrastination Habit

Nick Reynolds

D1795714

Table of Contents

My 5 Apps that you can use

Websites to help

My Final thoughts

Leave a Review

The trademarks that are used are without any consent, and the publication of the trademark is without permission or backing by the trademark owner. All trademarks and brands within this book are for clarifying purposes only and are the owned by the owners themselves, not affiliated with this document.

Disclaimer

Although the author and the publisher have made every effort to ensure that the information in this book was correct at press time, the author and publisher do not assume and hereby disclaim any liability to any party for any loss, damage, or disruption caused by error or omissions, whether such errors or omission result from negligence, accident or any other cause.

Your Free Gift

If you are not reading from an ebook you can select this link type this link in,

https://amzn.to/2IWoIx8 I'd like to give you a free gift for purchasing my book, it won't cost you a dime, it's *"The Abundance Magnet"*. This book shows you incredible ways of attracting just about anything you want in life, by the simple law of attraction. This will help you live the best life possible through attraction. You can Click here to Download Your Copy Now.

Procrastination Poetry

I'm thinking about thinking about retiring

    Not sure when that will be

I know I need to make a change

    I'll do it soon, you'll see

I'm thinking about thinking about moving

    To a warm place by the sea

Guess I'll do that another day

    It's dinnertime for me

I'm thinking about thinking about everything

    That I have to do

I suppose that I could start right now

    But...I'm off to the zoo

- Mike Gentile

"I'll write this tomorrow"

- Hidee Makayla

Introduction

Procrastination the killer of our dreams of four goals, isn't it. I always ask my clients, my friends, my colleagues, what can you do if you had better self-discipline? I mean, how much you could accomplish if you could just focus on one thing, and one thing only. I can bet you are thinking to yourself that you can accomplish a lot, so much more than your current output. So what really prevent us from doing this, so what really have us doing the things we hate over and over, getting the same results then hating ourselves?

There are many, which you can say contribute to our distraction, psychological, physiological and emotional. All of which can be addressed and resolve. One of the biggest poor habits that we have is called procrastination, procrastinating our lives away. We hate to do it, but we do it, and while we do it, we hate it. Can you see that we have a serious issue that needs to be addressed, and immediately.

As I have discussed in my previous book, *__The Procrastination Cure: Get Things Done__*

I discussed the many causes of procrastination, why we procrastination and how we can overcome these defects. The book focused on understanding procrastination and what is the root cause of this habit.

This book, however will focus solely on actions that you can take to beat the procrastination habit. The book goes in the different strategies that you can use to tackle and overcome procrastination and habits.

My story is one of triumph over adversity, triumph over poor habits and indiscipline. I was once a chronic procrastinator, procrastinating on everything, on all my goals, my dreams, and my passion. Eventually the time passed, drift away without me ever realizing it, just so quickly.

I found myself behind on my dream, behind on my goals, behind on my ambition. Afterwards you begin to come back to yourself and you ask yourself the question, was it worth it? Was my habit of procrastination worth it, the price I paid to give up on my dream, was it worth it, and the answer is a resounding NO!

 I found myself doing a 4 year degree in 6 years, I found myself in arrears on my goals, arrears on my dreams, arrears on my loan. I then come to realize that this is how people fail, this is what failure feels like. I then realize that if I do not change, I may be a bit ahead, but I will definitely still be behind on my goals. When I think about that I decided that I need to focus all my efforts on beating my bad procrastination habits, focus on being as productive as possible. I did not accomplish this through stressing myself out, but rather prioritizing effectively.

When you think of it, when you think of your job you may very well be doing as little work as the person at the top is doing, but maybe because they prioritize specific skill, certain habits, they have manage to developed themselves and do very well and climb up the ladder. As well, they may have just as well be lucky, know the boss or something. Either way you need to focus on your goals, and achieve what you said you would do. Goal achievement is not guaranteed, but pursuit of the goal and effort will greatly increase your chances.

I am sure many of us, including myself have asked the question, Am I a procrastinator? The answer to that question is a resounding yes, yes you are a procrastinator, and in fact we all are procrastinator. As I have said in my previous book, ***Procrastination Cure: Get things done,*** We all have at some point or another have procrastinated and we still do, as we are not machines, if we were not procrastinators, our lives would be chaotic. Just imagine, what are the weirdest things that you would do, if you just acted on your impulse? Maybe some of us would jump off a bridge or hit a friend in their face after strong words are exchanged, or tell our boss to piss off. So you see how procrastination is important for our survival at times.

However on the contrary, when we do too much procrastination, especially at those important times in our lives, the result is failure, regrets, depression, anxiety and missed deadlines. So we have to know how to manage the habit of procrastination carefully to be productive, and resourceful.

This book provide ways in which you can take actions, to break the habits that you have. It is the habit of procrastination that we need to take control of and not procrastination itself, this book will give you actionable strategies you can use to break habits, and also create new habits to replace them.

However let's go into some ways you can identify if you are a procrastinator.

1. If you find yourself waking up late, all the time especially for work, and other events, you are a procrastinator.

2. You sleep whenever, where ever, even in productive hours, you tend to sleep when you want to put off a task, or avoid doing a hard job. This happens a lot during college, high school and at home. We have a task and jobs to do, and we skip around them, sleep around them, and never do them.

3. When you find that a task is too hard you give up and do something easier, something that is less challenging and often times is not that important.

4. You now longer make commitment for anything, you tend to shy away from commitment as in the pass, you have fell short on your promises and commitments. You no longer trust yourself in the commitments that you are making. You have no regard for deadlines and important dates.

5. You have bad attitude toward people that work hard to reach their goals, especially people who are achieving more than you, outperforming your standards, you get sense of envy, as if why do they have to work so hard.

6. Your friends and co-workers complain about your slacking, sloppiness more than just once, or your group members if you are in school. Once you find that your co-workers and your friends are complaining about your work ethic you know by then, you have an issue.

7. You find yourself always rushing, always hurrying because of your poor time management skills. You wake up for work 6:30AM to leave by 7:00AM, somehow convince yourself you can eat, bathe, press and organize yourself in half an hour. I use to do this a lot, too much anxiety and horn blowing in traffic.

8. You only take actions, when you have to do something. You ever wonder why most person can stay 8hrs at a job, but not 4hrs on their dream they are trying to achieve? Because they don't have to do it, you have to stay at your job, but you don't have to chase your dreams. Once you find that you only take actions in a must do situation, you need to do some changing.

9. You spend a lot of time, dreaming, imagining how life will be, more time than actually doing what is required for you to achieve your goals.

10. You always wish to have more discipline, every day you beat yourself and say, if I just have more discipline I would be so much better off. None the less, you never do what you said you will, you never try to be more productive. You just go through the day the same way.

If you can identify yourself with any of what I explained above you may be a procrastinator, may not be chronic. As I explained in my previous book ***Procrastination Cure: Get things Done,*** we all at some point procrastinate, that is not the issue, the issue is when we become chronic procrastinators. That is when we really need to worry, in this book, we will speak directly to the action plans, the hacks, the resources that you can use to overcome this habit.

Setting Smart Goal

Smart goal is an acronym used to guide to set goals, the acronym is S.M.A.R.T, which stands for Specific, Measurable, Achievable, Relevant, and Time bound. The smart goals is used by many top management experts all over the world. A lot of the concepts were attributed to Peter Drucker's Management Objectives.

1. Specific, your goals should be clear and specific, it is super important that your goals are specific. When your goals are clear, you will be able to focus your efforts and feel truly motivated to achieve your goals. When you are looking to set specific goals, focus on what you want to accomplish, which resources can help you achieve your goals. This guideline will help you to refine your goals, which will help you achieve your goals.

2. Make sure that the goal is measureable, so that you can track your goals, and stay motivated, this will help you meet your deadlines and encourage you to stay on course. The questions you need to ask is how much, how many, and how will you know when you accomplish your goals.

3. You need to also make sure that your goals is achievable, you goals need to be realistic, attainable to be successful. You can set goals that stretch your horizons, but also is still within the realm of possibility. Make sure that when you are setting achievable goals, to not overlook resources that can help you attain that goal. You need to identify if the goal is achievable, if it can be accomplished as well, you do not want to set a goal that I impossible to achieve, like becoming a billionaire by next year.

4. The other step in setting smart goals, is to make sure that the goals are relevant to you, and that it also aligns with other relevant goals that you have. Make sure that the goal that you are going after means something to you, make sure that the end itself has important and meaning. Find if this goal is worthwhile, does it matches up with my needs, and is it the opportune time to do this. Ask yourself similar questions to these to find out if this goals is really necessary.

5. The next step in setting your goals is to make the goal time bound, have some sort of deadline to achieve in your goal, make it something to work toward, you can have weekly goals, then monthly goals.

S.M.A.R.T Goal into Action

Let us look at a few steps you would like to take to accomplish your SMART Goals. you can set smart goals for the year, month. or quarterly. I prefer quarterly, as it allows me to make necessary changes very quick.

Step One: Visualize what you want to focus on

Start with where you would want to be year from now. where you would want to be, what you want to do, how are you going to achieve this? Then work backwards, once you have a blueprint for where you want to be, all you have to do is reverse engineer. Start with visualization, start with seeing yourself as how where you would want to be. From this you will know how to set quarterly goals, working backword.

Step Two: Create Quarterly and Monthly Segmentation

Once you have set your annual goal, you want to then break down your annual goals, to quarterly goals, set specific milestone that you need to achieve which would indicate to you that you are on track to accomplish the annual goals. The one year plan that you set for yourself, is a bunch of small goals coming together to achieve a larger goal.

Step Three

The next step is to plan weekly review of your goals, and what have you been able to accomplish. In addition to your monthly milestone, focus as well on your weekly milestones. Once you are able to hit those milestones each week, you should be on track to accomplishments, to tell if you are on or off track.

Stronger Focus

A heavy dependence on how to beat procrastination, is your ability to focus, and zero in on your job, your tasks at hand. And we will go into a few ways how you can do this to develop better focus.

1. Calm down, before you begin your task, calm your brain, and take a few moments to be in a comfortable state and just calm down and breathe. You will notice that doing this will help you concentrate and focus on your ambitions. This will help you to prepare your brain ready to focus on the upcoming task at hand.

2. Focus your focus, you need to get a clear understanding of where your focus, attention and time should be directed towards. You need to take time to evaluate what it is that needs your time and attention, what jobs. what task, need your time and your attention. Once you have identify that, double down and focus on that specific task until it is complete.

3. Log out, quite down for a few, take some time out of your down. to just declutter your mind, and log out for a few minutes from your email, social media. Just focus on your task at hand, focus on your job, what it is that needs to be done, and switch off all distractions, and get things done.

4. You can listen to your favourite musician while you do, whatever it is that you are trying to do. Often when I am writing or doing house chores, I would get my music on and focus 110% on the job that I am doing. Playing music remove the monotony in boring tasks, it just helps to make the task less boring to do. In that way you will be able to focus and get more things done.

5. Stop all multitasking work, cancelling all diversity jobs, you want to focus on one task to completion. Often times we think that it is a great idea to do several things at once, let me be clear it is not. Sometimes I would eat my meals and read, I find that I spend more time on both, than if I were to focus on doing just one. Do one thing at a time, believe me it works, it really does. Not only that multitasking is not particular effective, it also causes more stress, it stresses you out more than you would expect.

6. Take occasional breaks to reward yourself, many of us we only have the capacity to stay focus for an hour or so, instead of diverting to something that is totally unrelated to your objectives, take breaks maybe every 2 hour, or every 50 minutes, take like a 15 minute brake, then get back focused on your objective and make it happen.

Do a Weekly Review Prepare for your review

Doing a weekly review is critical to beating procrastination, and seeing where you measure up in terms of the goals that you set for yourself. This will allow you to stay on track with your goals and objectives that you want to achieve.

Preparing for your review will help you have enough time to get go through your list thoroughly, and to be focus while you are doing so. You should have a dedicated time to for each week, it could be on the weekend, or maybe Sunday morning before you begin. I feel more comfortable doing this in the morning as the time is cooler and my brain is free. Make it a regular habit, mandatory to do, allow the review to become a habit, a ritual.

1. You can schedule your review on a calendar, allow yourself at least one to two hours to go over your goals, to achieve your objectives.
2. Make sure that you have no pending work to do, after the review, if you have anything urgent, get that out of the way first before you begin your weekly review. You want to remain focus while you are doing this.
3. Find a nice comfortable area that you can call home, relax in your cave, I prefer to do this, while I am under a tree, early in the morning, when a lot less people are up. Just inhale and exhale nature and begin my review of my week.

4. Make sure that when you are about the begin your weekly review, that you are not disturbed, that you are not distracted in any way, as you will be required to zone in and really internalise getting your goals accomplished.

5. Then after you have settled, and have reviewed your list, prepare action list on what you will do next to achieve your goal. Create a better action plan, identify where you left off, what you could have done better, what you are going to do about it.

Time Boxing

Time boxing is sampling fixing a specific time period to work on a group of tasks, or just one task. For me I used the first 2 hours in the morning to pray and look for new opportunity, then I used the remaining hours to write or work on my business. Instead of working on a task until it is done, you will work on that task specifically within that specific hour. I will further go into ways which you can use time boxing to get things done.

1. **Get Rid of Small Task,** This is a great way to get rid of those small tasks that you keep on your list every day. Tasks which you may consider to be insignificant and not take any actions on them. What persons do time and time again is put these mini task for last in their day, then they do not have enough time and mental energy to put any effort in them at the end. A great way to get these task done, is create a time box and tackle all of these task at once. Doing this will release the mental clutter that you have in your mind, and give you enough room to tackle the major task with more focus and efficiency.

2. **Quick Spurts for Creative Projects,** Creative projects often time depends on inspiration for them to be done effectively, such as school designer projects, writing a bestselling novel or even writing a song. These type of projects require immediate action once you have a burst of idea, execute these ideas immediately do not wait. A lot of time when we are seeking inspiration, or a creative idea, we have to give our brain the idea and let our subconscious brain handle the creative process.

3. **Be Strict on time,** if you are attempting to pursue a big goal, or a very important goal, be sure to make it time sensitive. Many times I find myself going after a goal, getting so distracted all the day have passed and I have accomplished nothing. I find it very disappointing when that happens, so what I often do is perform an audit, auditing what it is that I need to accomplish for the day. Then I would structure the day in time boxes. Make sure you do not get your day too full, eliminating unimportant task and focus in on what is truly important.

4. **Put important task first,** it's something we always hear but yet few of us do, to put our most important task first. For me that is prayer and worship before I begin my day. Then after prayer, I will get to my number one task which is working on my business, it may change from time to time. What you want to make certain of is that you put whatever it is that is most important for that day first on the list. Create a time box to accomplish this, before you are distracted by other things, because distraction can lead you down a whole different pathway away from your goal.

Break Big Task into Smaller Ones

I am sure you have heard of this before, it's kind of cliché but it works, and it will always work. When you have big jobs or task to do, stretch out those task into bite size, bits and pieces to get them done. this type of strategy works perfectly if you begin tasks and projects early out before the deadlines. For example if it is that you have a room to organise before you're the end of the week, or say a garage, first start by clearing out all to junk on one day, say day one. Then on day two focus on things in the garage that you don't necessarily need, then day three focus on putting the stuff that you need outside or on one side of the garage. Then begin cleaning, dusting etc. That is how you get your goals accomplished in bit size, and guess what? You will be so much more relieved when you approach your goal with this strategy.

Get in the Gym

If you have a serious interest to beating procrastination, you may need to also consider doing regular exercise. I find that for me going to the gym helps me stay more focused at work, and enjoy my work more. I feel a sense of rejuvenation and motivation when I do anything afterword's, I feel like an animal.

It is said by scientist that during the course of our life, as we age our body generates fewer and fewer brain cells and exercise is found to slow down that process.

Exercise is also found to energise your body during the day, which will help you to knock off that lethargic feeling, we sometime experience. Giving us the energy we need to do activities which are important to us, the one that will push us closer to our goals. Our cells contain a component known as mitochondria which is known to energize the cells in the body, the more energy you have the more you are motivated to get things done. Doing the exercises will give your body what we consider to be a high, runners high which is immediate, enough to get you off your butt and do what you need to.

Research have found that doing regular exercise help you to feel better in yourself and stay happier, allowing you to have a more positive attitude throughout the course of the day.

No Multitasking

It is very tempting to do some sort of multitasking when you are after your goals, or you are simply just trying to get a task done, or finish. Such as while you are doing the laundry, you are doing the dishes, or you are tuning the car. It seem so cool and so productive and it just makes so much sense to do. However multiple studies have shown that multitasking will actually kill your level of productivity.

Once you find yourself switching from task to task, it takes up to 25 minutes to get your brain back to focus 100% on that specific job. Switching your brain from task to task, actually creates distraction, and destroys your level of focus. While you may think that you can do many things at once and make a big dent in your goals, actually it may reduce your productivity, some studies have shown that, this sometime can be up to 40%. I know that for a fact that when I focus deeply on a task, I will get more stuff done, a staggering amount. What I think I could have done in 3 hours I did it in 1 hour. So make sure that once you are getting down and dirty knocking out those goals, to actually stay focus on one and one only, to finish.

To Do List

If you are serious about breaking your procrastination habit, you have to have a to do list, you just have to, it is an absolute must that you create a to do list. This will help you stay focus as you go along, this will assist you to not waste time on unfruitful task, or frivolous matters. Having a to do list is like putting on your blinders and charging forward without distraction, and do not go outside of your list unless you have to. Once you have check off the task on your list, you can move on with your life without any form of guilt or anxiety. Having the confidence that you have done all that you need to do.

Having a to do list helps you prioritize, the to do list will ensure that you focus on the most important task, be sure that you do not give into the doing the least important task first. This is still a form of procrastination, get into a practice of knocking out important task first thing, then relax and easy and do your other tasks.

Sticking to Deadlines

Using deadlines will help boost your productivity in a major way. I use it to kick my own self in the butt to stay focus and get more results. Having a deadline will give you an idea as to what projects are important and which projects do not require so much attention. If you know that you have a project or task to finish on a specific day, maybe at the end of the week, it makes it easier for you to decline other offers to engage in other projects.

Setting a deadlines give you the chance of completing task, with enough times for contingencies. When you get a deadline from the office often time, it is before the actually date needed, because your manager know that, there has to be some room for contingency plans, simply because things happen. For example, not doing an important project the day before its schedule deadline date, then you find that you need to print copies to present in a meeting. only to encounter a defective printer. I see this so many time. did it as well many times over.

When we work with a deadline, we know that we do not have much time to waste or spare, so we plug away doing our job to get it done before the deadline have pass. Set up penalties if the job you are doing is a personal goals, put it on yourself if you joke around and didn't meet your goals. Once we can put ourselves in that level of focus our productivity will soar through the roof.

When we're working against a deadline, we know that we don't have time to spare; if something is due at 3pm and we just wolfed down our lunch, we simply can't afford to waste time. The result is that we're a lot more diligent about ignoring the little time-wasters that would usually derail us.

You know what I mean: we ignore the non-urgent phone calls and emails, and push to get the work done. We don't get hung up on the little nit-picky details that deep down we know nobody cares about — we just plough through.

In other words, we make the best use we can of the time we have. This is basically the definition of productivity!

2 Minute Rule

The two minute rule is basically getting done whatever task that you can do it two minute, immediately. Often time we do not take actions on certain task because they are insignificant, but if you can get this done in less than two minute, do it right away. It will amaze you how much you can do when, you apply that rule, and how much things you put off until it get so overwhelming to do.

Any new task or new habit that you wish to take on, just have it settled in your mind that you are going to just dedicate two minute to do as much as you can do. Often time you will find yourself going much more than two minutes, even hours. The key is to teach yourself to start, once you start you will develop the momentum you need to finish and do more. The key inside the two minute rule is not to focus on actually finishing the task but more so beginning the task, getting the ball rolling. Once you can begin you can finish, believe me when I say that.

Delegate

Learn how to properly delegate task and jobs to person to achieve results faster, I do this a lot especially when I have a lot to do. In this age and time, there are many task you can outsource to persons online. Such as writing and updating your resume, creating a website, or writing contents for a blog post. Task like these you can pay persons to do online, or locally.

In fact task such as grocery shopping, or picking up medical goods, can be outsourced as well. you do have several companies in your local area that provide these services. As well services such as home cleaning, washing, organising the home, all these jobs can be delegated and outsource to persons. if it is that you believe you do not have the time, or as well, if you are procrastinating on the issue. and would like to just get it over with. Jobs such as cleaning the garage which everyone hates can be outsourced as well, to free up your time to do things that are more meaningful.

Delegating/Outsourcing a task is an excellent way of beating procrastination and getting results that you need to achieve your goals. If you find that a specific job may be actually taking too much out of you. you can even ask your friends. or your family and children to help, or just delegate the specific task to them. Doing this will help you further stay focus and committed to the other things. Just remember whenever you are overwhelmed delegate the job.

Eating an Elephant

How do you eat an elephant? I will wait on your response..One bite at a time. The first time I heard this statement I thought it was funny, as well. I thought it was really meaningful. I remember back in University when I was trying to finish up 27 courses, it felt so overwhelming and challenging. but I did 3 every semester. then finally the 27 turned the 11, then 11 turn to 7 then 3. After all of that I finally completed my education. looking back the goal seem so out of reach. so never ending. but finally it was finished.

That is how we should tackle every large task that we are given, the task that seem so impossible, so overwhelming. Take it on one step at a time. inch by inch it's a cinch. by a yard it's hard, you find that when you look at your goals from that stand point, it becomes much easier to accomplish. For me writing this book, I set a daily budgeted time of a 1000 words per day, over a week a month it adds up, and that may just take 2 or 3 hours to do. Just imagine if I had just told myself that this book should be 20,000 words, imagine my mind set, and imagine how that will affect my psychology. It makes a big difference.

So when you are faced with a decision to make, when doing a large task, take it one step at a time, look at it inch by inch, step by step, visualizing how easier it is to get it done. Taking on your goals in bite size, day by day, minute by minute, this makes a world of difference.

Temptation Bundling

This is something I am doing right now, what is that you may ask, this is where you connect something that you don't want to do, with something that you enjoy. Example what I am doing now is writing while I am playing music and watching the television.

You need to ensure that you have to pair the wanted action with the unwanted action simultaneously. Ensure that you can only engage in the pleasure if you take the unwanted action. The concept of temptation bundling is coupling the jobs that you have with something that you enjoy and can do simultaneously. For instance while you are at the gym, you can watch entertainment stations or online channels, why do you think they have music in the gym and flat screen television everywhere you go, solely because of keeping person motivated while they go through their rigorous workouts.

This strategy is used to build healthier more productive habits and activities, this strategy uses instant gratification, and while having the benefits of being productive which is more productive in the long run, with no downsides.

My 5 Apps that you can use

<u>Detox Procrastination Blocker</u>

This app works as a timer that lock you from messing with your phone when you are doing important task. Most times we are distracted by notifications that cause us to tamper with our phones. Once you download the app, simply open the app and you will see a timer on the main page. You can set the timer for the length of time you want your apps to be disabled. The app will also prompt you asking you to confirm your actions. The thing with <u>Detox</u> is that once you lock the device it is lock, nothing will enable you to open the device, so only use this when you are ready to deep dive in some work.

Procraster

This app is compatible for IPhone and the IPad, I am sorry for to say for android users. When you download this app, you have option of selecting whether "My task is too big" and "I don't know where to start", "I've made a mistake" the app will then make recommendation based on the answer. For example if you chose "I don't know where to start", the app will respond in a way to break down the project in parts which will encourage you to complete it.

You can also check statistics in the app, over time, which will show you your progress that will provide extra motivation for you to keep going.

You can check their website out for more information, this is probably one of the best app that I have seen out there in the marketplace.

Wunderlist

Wunderlist help you manage your to do list, it removes the overwhelming feeling of having too much to do. To do lists help us to prioritize important task that need to be accomplished, it sets reminders to keep us on target with our goals and objectives.

You have the option to set due dates and reminder and assign to dos, these reminders help you not forget important deadlines.

Todoist

Being as human as we forget stuff, I do as well, especially if we are overwhelmed with activities in our natural live. What this app will assist us with is setting up a TODO List, this app we can all benefit from it. With this app you can track task, sync the across devices, which will help you in staying on course with your task and jobs. You can definitely check out this app, if you are serious about getting over procrastination definitely take a look at this.

Freedom

Freedom reduce distraction, making it easier for you to stay focus on the task at hand. A lot of time we procrastinate when we can easily switch from task to task. Freedom prevent access to the internet at your specify time, blocking access to email, and social

media networks. Very useful for person with the social media bug, like myself. So try it out,

it can really change the way how you do things and your productivity.

Websites to help

Stickk

Stickk is a very innovative but familiar, this site ensure that you have some form of accountability. You can make your goal public, so other people will see and identify if you done what you set out to do or not. You have a timeline, set up some stakes get some likeminded people to rally on with you on the course to success. The community that you are a part of can help you stay accountable to your goal, this is worth the experience. They have data driven tools,that help to reshape behavior.

Keepmeout

This site is perfect for those of us, who while using our computer cannot seem to stay off the different social media networks and websites we love to hate. The website allows you to create a link add the link as a bookmark in your browser, so whenever you are going on the website, the site will give you an alert that you made a commitment to not visit that specific site. It is a great tool to have if you are serious about achieving your goals. It's lesser of a website and more so a tool, the tool is very easy to use.

RescueTime

Rescue time is an online tracking tool that shows you how much time you spend on different website. The site will tally up the information, and provide feedback in data format, that you can use to make a thorough evaluation on what you need to get rid of to do more. Once you discover how much time you are wasting, I am sure you will stop immediately.

RescueTime

RescueTime tracks how you use your time online and on applications on your computer so you can see how much time you're actually wasting. Once you see it, you'll stop wasting time almost immediately. However this website, there is a charge for $9.00, but if you are serious about your goal, you will get it done.

MeeTimer

Me timer is a powerful extension that you can install in your firefox browser to provide you with the data of what you are spending most of your time on. This extension that you can install in your browser monitors your time online, and provide feedback statistically in a form that you can easily understand and grasp. Allowing you to stay focus and reduce wastage of time.

My Final thoughts

If I can do it, you can do it, as I said in the beginning of the book, you cannot totally get rid of procrastination. What you have to focus on is decrease your habit of procrastination more and more over time. And yes you find yourself procrastination on things that are important, but do not let that be to your detriment, if you have a paper due next week, begin, if you have the chores to do, start. Think about it, if you have to do something, why wait, why not just get it out the way, free your mind and goof off afterwords. When you do this you feel better, more accomplished and more productive, it will have a tremendous effect on your body.

Leave a Review

The next thing I would like to say is, if you find this book rewarding in any way, PLEASE LEAVE A REVIEW, honest review. Or share it with your friends, this may help someone overcome the challenge they have with procrastination. Thank You

Printed in Great Britain
by Amazon

14040699R00027